Bread for the ducks

Story by Beverley Randell
Illustrations by Betty Greenhatch

Jack and Billy and Mom
went down to the river
to see the ducks.

3

"Here is the bread

  for the ducks," said Mom.

"I like bread," said Billy.

"No, Billy," said Jack.

"The bread is not for you."

"Here come the ducks,"
said Jack.

"They look hungry,"
said Mom.

Jack said to the ducks,

"Here you are.

Here is some bread for you."

9

Billy looked at the bread.

"I am hungry, too," he said.

"Look!" said Jack.

"Here come some little ducklings.

They like bread, too.

Come down here, Billy."

12

13

"Oh, Billy!" said Mom.

"Where is the bread?"

15

"Here you are, little ducklings,"
said Billy.
"This is for you."

16